THE
AMERICAN CIVIL WAR
RECREATED IN
COLOUR PHOTOGRAPHS

DR. DAVID TH.
SCHILLER

Windrow & Greene
London

© David Th. Schiller
Published in Great Britain 1990 by
Windrow & Greene Ltd.
19 Floral Street
London WC2E 9DS

Printed in Singapore

Reprinted 1994

British Library Cataloguing in Publication Data
Schiller, David T.
    The American Civil War recreated in colour
    photographs.
    (Europa – militaria).
    1. American Civil War
    I. Title   II. Series
    973.7

ISBN 1-872004-40-7

Author's note: The following organisations arrange
re-enactments and 'living history' events in Europe,
and through them readers may contact the various
Civil War interest groups. These associations also
have contacts with Civil War groups in the USA,
where the hobby is so diversified that no federal
association exists.

Great Britain
Southern Skirmish Association
M. Freeman
136 Snakes Lane
Woodford Green
Essex IG8 7HZ

American Civil War Society
c/o Bill Davies
54 Rowland Close
Warrington, Cheshire
WA2 0DQ

Germany
Arbeitsgemeinschaft Geschichte Live (AGL) e. V.
c/o Karl-Heinz Speicher
Richard Wagner Str. 8
6636 Überherrn

France
Club Confederé de France
21 Boulevard Poniatowski
75012 Paris

A Trip in Time

THE DESPERATE CLIMAX was at hand. For two days now the Army of Northern Virginia had hurled itself against the blue-clad lines of the Army of the Potomac around the small Pennsylvania town of Gettysburg. Now, on this third day, General Robert E. Lee had assembled the troops of his subordinate generals Pickett, Pettigrew and Trimble, and aimed them like a fist at the centre of the union line on Cemetery Ridge. All the Confederate artillery batteries were drawn together to lend their support. The three divisions formed up; and then broke from their cover — perfect lines of infantry in gray and butternut, battalion by battalion, brigade by brigade, drums rolling, flags snapping in the wind. On they came, their ranks thinning as they suffered casualties all the way up the slope, closing on the low wall lined with a dark blue mass of troops from Pennsylvania, New York, Massachusetts, Ohio and Vermont. As the confederates struggled towards the enemy line — an insignificant field wall which would go down in history as 'the high-water mark of the Confederacy' — the salvoes from the Union troops grew and merged into a wall of fire. Brigadier Armistead and some 150 of his men finally clawed their way up to it, but only to be engulfed in moments. It was all over: the last gamble had failed . . .

But it was not a July day in 1863. This battle was fought in 1988, under the eyes of hundreds of thousands of spectators; and when the last shot had echoed away the 10,000 participants in this final battle of the three-day Gettysburg anniversary re-enactment stood up, wiped off the sweat, grime and theatrical blood, and shook hands with their foes. And then they uncovered their heads and bent their knees where they stood; and as they remembered those who had suffered and died for their cause in those fields 125 years before, an eerie silence descended over the whole battlefield, where moments before thousands of men had screamed war-cries, and thousands of guns had thundered. Now the only sound was the flapping of battle-flags in the wind; until, from one end of the field, the plaintive sound of a bugle rose into the summer sky. As the heartbreaking notes of 'Taps' mourned over the old battlefield, many a man had tears in his eyes; I was there, and I wept with them.

Those three days at Gettysburg were not only an emotional climax, but for thousands of people the crowning point of years of effort and preparation, of study and training; the culmination of all they had hoped to gain in return for the hard work and expense demanded by the hobby of historical re-enactment. More than once during that series of marches, skirmishes and battles the ultimate goal of re-enacting was reached: that fleeting moment when a level of authenticity is achieved which really does transport the participant back in time. At such moments, if only for a few

seconds, I had a direct encounter with history: as one of my friends from Virginia put it, 'The door opened, and I stepped through it into that other time'.

A fitting vindication of the re-enactment hobby can be found in the words of one of those men who actually did take part in the War Between the States. Berry Benson, from North Carolina, wrote in his *Reminiscences*: 'Who knows but it may be given to us, after this life, to meet again in the old quarters, to play chess and draughts, to get up soon to answer the morning rollcall, to fall in at the tap of the drum for drill and dress parade, and again hastily don our war gear while the monotonous patter of the long roll summons to battle? Who knows but again the old flags, ragged and torn, snapping in the wind, may face each other and flutter, pursuing and pursued, while the cries of victory fill the summer day? And after the battle, then the slain and wounded will arise, and all will meet together under the two flags, all sound and well, and there will be talking and laughter and cheers, and all will say: Did it not seem real? Was it not as in the old days?'

History as a Hobby

Re-enacting — or 'Living History', as some prefer to call it — is an active encounter with the past. Those involved with this pastime recreate bygone days, through playing out specific historical episodes with authentic clothing and equipment, in order to further our understanding of historical developments which still influence us today. Such an undertaking demands intensive research into the period chosen, to achieve a detailed knowledge of costume, accoutrements, military drill, characteristic behaviour, and a hundred different facets of day-to-day life. It demands long and dedicated work, and considerable expense for the individual. So popular has this pastime become that today there are active Living History groups devoted to periods ranging from the days of Imperial Rome through the Middle Ages, the English Civil War, the American Revolution, the Napoleonic Wars, to the two World Wars. Yet it all started with the re-enactment of episodes from those four bloody years, 1861-65, which historians (depending upon where their sympathies lie) now call either the American Civil War, the War Between the States, the Second Revolution, the War for Southern Rights, or the Latest Unpleasantness . . .

Few other historical conflicts have so captured and held men's imagination. The heroism and the romance of those Civil War years have always fascinated Americans, and with them the rest of the English-speaking world. Even when the war was still fresh in the memories of those who suffered through it, participants and their families and friends flocked in their tens of thousands to the annual reunions of Civil War veterans' associations. During one of these, in November 1903, the first Civil War battle re-enactment took place: 430 Confederate survivors of William Mahone's Brigade formed a column of companies in the streets of Petersburg as they had done in July 1864, when the Union engineers had blown a huge mine under one of the Confederate forts. As in the actual 'Battle of the Crater', Mahone's veterans followed Col. Stewart of the 61st Virginia in a charge on the earthworks, their hearty 'Rebel yell' echoed by the applause of thousands of spectators.

In the decades that followed the US Army, Marine Corps, and various National Guard units staged re-creations of Civil War engagements on the barren and depopulated Virginia battlefields in modern uniform, firing blank rounds from rifles and even machine guns; some of these events were mounted as actual manoeuvres, others were purely public spectacles. The climax of these early endeavours came with the 75th anniversary dates in 1936-37 when Army and Marine regular and cadet formations refought the battle of Manassas, Chancellorsville, the Crater and Gettysburg. But a

above

For them the war was real: well-equipped Michigan Volunteer Infantry standing at 'parade rest' for the photographer. (Library of Congress)

The long blue line: the National Regiment, an amalgamation of various Northern re-enactment groups who came together to form a large unit for the 1988 Gettysburg event, stand in line for morning roll-call.

larger conflict already darkened the horizon, and World War II brought these pageants to an end.

Twenty-five years later interest in the War Between the States was rekindled by a new generation of history buffs. On 28 May 1950 a handful of men from the shooting clubs of two small neighbouring towns in Maryland went out for a friendly target match with original Civil War muzzle-loading rifles. To complete their outfits they donned 'bummer's caps', John Wayne-style bib front shirts, belts with 'US' and 'CS' plates, and contemporary cartridge boxes. The shooting match proved quite successful; the event — won by eight Confederates calling themselves the 'Norfolk Long Rifles' — drew a good crowd, and it was decided to stage similar shoots once in a while.

Within six years the idea had caught on with so many black powder enthusiasts that no regular club range could accommodate all those interested in competing. An organisation was founded with the title 'North-South Skirmish Association' (N-SSA); and two annual weekend events, in spring and fall, were organised on Army ranges. Apart from the musket shoot-outs, similar matches took place for breech-loading carbines, cap-and-ball revolvers, and — last but not least — half-scale and full-scale field pieces.

The Centennial of the Civil War in 1961 generated a new wave of interest.

The opening re-enactment of the anniversary, at the original Battlefield National Park of Manassas on 22/23 July 1961 drew more than 2,500 participants, most of them from the N-SSA; firing blank rounds, they manoeuvred for the delighted entertainment of some 50,000 spectators. By today's standards those early re-enactments were far from authentic: blue jeans with sewn-on yellow 'cavalry stripes', checkered polyester shirts and gaudy, overdecorated officers' uniforms were still the order of the day. But while some participants employed Indian Wars period Springfield 'trap-door' breech loaders (or even semi-automatic Garands!), most at least used the original Civil War muskets and revolvers which were then still readily and inexpensively available.

In the past 30 years re-enactment has come of age. The 'gonzo' re-enactors of the 1960s, with their careless approximations of costume, are no more; and the 125th anniversary battle series, 1986-90, proved that Living History had grown from a light-hearted weekend party in the open air to a professionally performed art. Security consciousness had been raised to such a high standard that even in huge encounters like Gettysburg 1988, where 12,000 armed men took the field, no serious accidents occurred.

Authenticity has become the watchword. This pastime is no longer just a weekend frolic; groups now spend many hours researching the history of the units which they represent down to the smallest detail. Blue jeans and synthetic-fibre clothing are definitely out: the state-of-the-art re-enactor's

Sunset over Antietam battlefield, and one of many regimental memorials which mark that bloodiest of days: 17 September 1862, when more Americans fell dead or wounded than on any other day of that or any other of America's wars — 12,400 Union and 13,700 Confederate soldiers. Lee won a tactical victory, but suffered a strategic defeat in that McClellan's Army of the Potomac forced him to abandon his first invasion of the North.

Silent vigil: a Union sentry overlooks the Antietam cornfields from his guard position, perhaps imagining the heavy losses suffered by Hooker's dawn attack which passed through here on the way to the Dunkard church.

Gettysburg today: as he did on the fateful 2 June 1863, the lifesize statue of Kemble Warren, then Chief Topographical Engineer of the Army of the Potomac, looks out over the battlefield from Little Round Top — the rocky hill which formed the southern anchor of the Union line, and which was the scene of bitter fighting.

self-esteem rests on his exactly authentic uniform and accoutrements, on which he may spent hundreds of dollars. While much is still hand- and home-made, to authentic period patterns, more and more clothing and equipment is being turned out professionally — from percussion cap pouches, to A-shaped infantry tents — by a growing 'cottage industry' catering to the needs of the discriminating re-enactor. Far from being polyester, his uniform is now quite likely to be hand-sewn from cloth specially woven to resemble mid-19th century fabrics even if viewed under a magnifying glass.

The number of participants in these events has also multiplied: in the USA alone it is estimated that some 50,000 people are now actively involved in one form of Living History or another. Well-established groups exist in every state from Alaska to Florida. Re-enactments are not limited to the actual Civil War locations; although there are a host of events every year up and down the eastern states, the summer tourist may be surprised to find blue and gray ranks battling for 'Gettysburg' in front of the California State Capitol in Sacramento. What used to be small, localised events like the little battle of Olustee in northern Florida have grown to become national attractions: now participants from as far away as Indiana, New York, and

Then and now: the sunken road below Marye's Heights at Fredericksburg. In this natural defensive position Thomas Cobb's Georgia brigade repulsed vigorous Union attacks by Winfield Scott Hancock's division on 13 December 1862. The Irish Brigade formed from the 63rd, 69th and 88th New York Volunteers, along with the 28th Massachusetts and 166th Pennsylvania, were decimated in this attack. Most of the men were immigrants, many of whom had been deported from Ireland to Tasmania for rebellion against the British crown. The Confederate General Longstreet later described the Union dead piled three deep in front of this wall.

even Europe fly in to enjoy the spring warmth of the southernmost state.

Only a few of the men in blue and butternut still carry original weapons. The replica industry was started in Italy in the late 1950s by American entrepreneurs like Turner Kirkland of the Dixie Gun Works, and Val Forgett of Navy Arms. The first slow trickle of working reproduction black powder arms has grown into a steady stream of different models. As well as rifles and carbines in various configurations, such as the Sharps and Smith breech-loaders, the whole range of Enfield pattern Minié rifles, and the 1861 and 1863 Springfields, a variety of well-made handguns is now available, from the .36 Navy Colt to the mighty LeMat 'grapeshot revolver'.

Official recognition has not been withheld from these efforts. Publications such as *Newsweek*, *National Geographic*, and even the *Wall Street Journal* have devoted space to this new national enthusiasm. Video films taken at the 125th anniversary battles are used in schools to educate youngsters about their nation's history. These days the US National Park Service, as well as numerous museums, make increasing use of re-enactment groups for their holiday interpretation programmes. Even the Hollywood film moguls recognise the value of so much knowledge and enthusiasm: when the TV mini-series *The Blue and the Gray* and *North and South* were filmed hundreds

Commemorating those who fought and died: Union artillery re-enactors from New York place a wreath at the Gettysburg battlefield marker of their original battery.

A lonely grave at Ball's Bluff is the last resting place of Pennsylvania Col. Edward D. Baker, buried on the Virginia side of the Potomac when he fell during a small-scale raid on 21 October 1861. An ex-congressman and a close friend of Abraham Lincoln, his pointless death during what was meant to be a slight demonstration against the confederate outposts on the river greatly grieved the President.

In a National Park outside Richmond, Union re-enactors demonstrate the infantry drill — here, 'support arms' stance — to summer tourists. The soldier at right has the crossed axes sleeve insignia of a pioneer.

of re-enactors were enlisted for 50 dollars a day each to serve in the battle scenes. The praised authenticity of the Oscar-nominated film *Glory* owes much to the same pool of historical expertise.

Civil War re-enactment is not limited to the USA anymore. British history buffs were the first to pick up the re-enactment 'bug'; the fever has now spread all over Europe, and had even infected individuals as far distant as Australia and New Zealand. It is understandable that this should have happened, since the Civil War was far from being a purely American concern. In more than one way it involved the European nations as well — first and foremost Britain, whence weapons, clothing, ships, money, and even a degree of political support came for the embattled South. Even so, some 60,000 Englishmen and Canadians served in the Union army. Indeed, immigrants filled the ranks of both armies. Next to the Irish, who were, with about 150,000, the largest foreign-born contingent, the Germans formed the most important ethnic minority: such famous Union units as Berdan's Sharpshooters and the 1st NY Cavalry were founded by Germans. In the South many regiments from states such as Virginia and Texas were recruited from Teutonic immigrants and their descendants.

Most of the European clubs today have strong links with re-enactment organisations in the USA. On both sides of the Atlantic, all walks of life are represented in their ranks — military men and civilians, teachers and students, clerks and craftsmen, journalists and policemen, civil servants and labourers. Their backgrounds are as diverse as their personal reasons for donning a uniform and shouldering a musket. Interest in human and military history is one, but not the only driving force behind this international movement. Escapism — simply a romantic glorification of the past? Perhaps . . . but don't we all dream sometimes of another world, in which honour and loyalty were not just words to be scoffed at?

previous page
Re-enactment is not all battles, parades, and solemn commemoration; part of the satisfaction comes from rustic camp life, from awakening to the early morning sun and the smell of the coffee already brewing. A woodland camp stirs during the 1986 Olustee event.

In a rare, unselfconscious period photograph, Union infantrymen are shown eating their meagre breakfast. Though most of the faces are young, the casual uniforms suggest that this is a seasoned, campaign-wise unit. (Library of Congress)

Infantry —
The Queen of Battles

FOR OBVIOUS REASONS, the great majority of re-enactors are 'footsloggers'. The expense and the special difficulties of re-creating authentically the appearance of cavalry and artillery put them beyond the reach of most individuals; but a keen re-enactor can turn himself into a convincing infantry rifleman for a few hundred dollars — and many hours of study and practice. When the hobby was in its 1960s infancy it was still possible to find original Union jackets for less than $50, and rifle-muskets for less than $100. Now, for high-quality reproduction items which will pass the merciless scrutiny of organisers at major events, an infantry re-enactor needs to spend about $200 on his basic uniform, $160 on personal equipment, and $250 on a rifle-musket.

In some ways the difficulties facing organisers of major re-enactments echo those of the staff officers who were faced in 1861 with turning enthusiastic masses of volunteers into effective regiments. History records the general ambivalence of free-born Americans towards military discipline; the tendency of small local unions to resist being submerged into the

The sheer numbers of men which can be put into the field at a major re-enactment event have a great deal to do with the overall conviction of the scene. Here the 5th New York — 'Duryea's Zouaves', named after their commander — lead a Union column out to battle at Manassas. On that single day in July 1861 the gaudily-uniformed 5th NY lost 117 killed out of 490 combatants.

larger units which efficiency demanded; and the high proportion of would-be officers . . . It is a tribute to the patience and dedication of the leading figures in the hobby that these difficulties have so often been overcome.

The first major event of the 125th anniversary series, in July 1986, was a good example of how these things can be achieved. 'Fourth Bull Run' (following the original battle of First Manassas or Bull Run in July 1861, the second battle in August 1862, and the first re-enactment in 1961) was organised by the American Civil War Commemorative Committee. The ACWCC was formed largely from leading members of groups such as the Stonewall Brigade, 5th New York, 14th Tennessee, 28th Massachusetts, Sykes' Regulars, the Ladies' Eastern Gunboat Society and the Culpeper Cavalry Museum.

The ACWCC found a battle site close to the original ground; the latter

Drawn up for inspection at the 125th anniversary of First Manassas, Company G of the 9th Virginia Volunteers — the 'Portsmouth Rifle Company' — wear their ante-bellum style dark blue militia uniform with green 'rifle' trim and white leather accoutrements.

The French 'Zouave' uniform style, characterised by a tasselled fez, baggy trousers, cummerbund, and short jacket worn open over a real or simulated vest, was popular among pre-war American militia. The fashion was inspired by the fame won in the Crimean War by France's colonial troops from Algeria. New York alone boasted some 33 Zouave-style volunteer regiments, of which the 5th — recreated here — was probably the most authentically French-looking. The 5th NY became celebrated both for its disciplined drill and its bravery in battle; but it was badly mauled by the Texas Brigade both in the Peninsula Campaign and at Second Bull Run. Note the sword worn by the sergeant, a normal distinction of that rank in the Union army.

With the colorguard leading, Gen. 'Stonewall' Jackson's Virginia Brigade step out in the early morning mist for their march to the Manassas battlefield, in July 1986.

The South had its share of exotically-clad militia outfits; the 1st Louisiana Special Battalion, more popularly known as 'Wheat's Zouaves' or the 'Tiger Zouaves', were represented at the Manassas 125th anniversary meeting. The original regiment was largely recruited from Irish immigrants in New Orleans.

was owned by the National Park Service, who were still unwilling to allow re-enactments there following the less than satisfactory behaviour of some 1961 re-enactors. The Committee set rigid standards of costume and equipment, and enforced them by inspection and the issue of graded passes. They organised the different participating groups into re-creations of 27 Union and 26 Confederate infantry battalions (apart from cavalry and artillery units). The painstaking process of dividing and amalgamating produced roughly similar units of about 85 men to represent each battalion, without major uniform anachronisms, and with only two colours; three

Firing by file: the Louisiana Tigers practice the complicated drill of a rolling company volley, in which only the two men in each file fire at the same time, the fire passing down the ranks in a rolling sequence of firing and reloading. In the deafening noise and smoke-blurred confusion of actual combat such demanding drill usually went by the board after a few volleys.

'officers' were allowed for units of 35 men and up, two for units with 25 to 35 men, and one for smaller units.

In all some 3,880 infantrymen took part in 'Fourth Bull Run'; and despite the major and unavoidable weakness of all Living History endeavours — the fact that discipline among civilian volunteers can only be achieved by self-regulation and unofficial peer group pressure — the resulting re-enactment set standards of authentic spectacle, and safety, which impressed everyone who attended.

Under their battle-worn flags, New York and Pennsylvania infantry of the 2nd Corps, 1st Division prepare for the Confederate assault against the Gettysburg line during the 1988 anniversary event.

Far south of the rolling hills of rural Pennsylvania, a well–equipped Confederate volunteer photographed at the February 1986 Olustee Festival wears the large Mexican War era forage cap popular with many Southern militia units.

The Olustee meeting recreates the battle of February 1864 in northern Florida, and takes place on the original battlefield, now a state park. Thanks to the splendid organisation, including such luxuries as a mass catering service, Olustee has become one of the most popular annual events in the United States re-enactment calendar.

Prepared for anything: Confederates of the Department of the Gulf waiting to join battle at Olustee. True to historical practice, the bearded soldier has fixed to his hat a piece of paper bearing his name and his family's address so that his next-of-kin can be informed if he falls in battle.

below
One of the climactic moments of every year's re-enactment comes when a regiment (here the 7th Florida) forms square to fend off advancing Union cavalry, only to be smashed apart a few minutes later by hastily drawn up artillery.

overleaf
Enemy in sight! A skirmish line of the 7th Florida advances to contact through the swamplands of the Olustee battlefield.

A battle-worn veteran, wearing the red cloverleaf badge of W.S. Hancock's 2nd Corps, 1st Division on his battered 'bummer's cap' is brought to convincing life by a Californian 'Living History' enthusiast.

This soldier, 'taking five' near the Army Headquarters at Gettysburg, recreates the well-dressed Confederate of 1863. Army issue clothing — when it arrived at all — tended to wear out quickly on campaign. Captured Union items and civilian clothing were always in evidence in the Southern ranks. The only vaguely regulation uniform item here is the gray shell-jacket faced with infantry light blue.

Gettysburg, 1988: the Union army's National Regiment passes through camp in column of fours. The white disc worn on the caps identifies Pennsylvania troops of the 1st Corps, 2nd Division.

A unit which has always excited the imagination of history buffs and re-enactors alike was the 1st US Sharpshooters commanded by the flamboyant and controversial Hiram Berdan. The first companies of this outfit of élite riflemen were recruited from among German and Swiss shooting clubs in New York state. The weapon carried by these crack shots was the specially made Sharps breech-loading rifle with double-set trigger; here a Sharpshooter sergeant lectures his men on the finer points of a modern-day replica. His red diamond cap badge identifies the 3rd Corps, 1st Division. The regulation uniform, in rifle green trimmed with lighter green, was not universal on campaign; there is evidence that some men wore standard blue 'sack coats' and sky blue trousers, with only the cap and such trimmings as NCOs chevrons and trouser stripes in the official green shade.

The temperature during the First Manassas 125th anniversary event, 17–21 July 1986, reached the high 90s Fahrenheit, and some 400 participants and spectators collapsed from the oppressive heat — re-enactment can sometimes be distressingly realistic. Here Confederate reserves receive much-needed refreshments from one of more than 1,200 lady 'camp followers' who took part.

Drill, drill, and drill again . . . At the Manassas event two days were set aside for drills and manoeuvres before the actual battle was joined. With small groups from all over the country assembling into regiments for the re-enactment, and with such a high premium on safety, relentless practice was essential. Here Confederate volunteers including 'Louisiana Tigers' are drilled by a veteran wearing the old Mexican War period cap and accoutrements with which many Southern units marched off to war in 1861.

First Manassas anniversary, 1986: Union regiments file past the colorguard of the 11th New York Volunteers, the 'Fire Zouaves'. Only in the United States can re-enactment groups assemble numbers like this, to recreate convincingly the appearance of whole formed regiments. 'Fourth Bull Run' — as the 1986 Manassas re-enactment was quickly christened — drew no less than 6,100 costumed re-enactors.

'Turncoats': large organised re-enactments such as Manassas often require some units to abandon their traditional regimental identities in order to represent a different unit which was present at the original battle. In 1986 various groups from Florida and Georgia formed up to act as the 2nd and 4th South Carolina Infantry. Many more Confederates were expected than Union units, and the organisers were nervous that they might have to summon the courage to ask Confederates to act as Yanks for the day . . . In the event this ordeal was avoided by a generous voluntary gesture on the part of the First Provisional Brigade.

Turning point, Manassas, 20 July 1986: the Union advance seen in the distance is checked by the arrival of Confederate reinforcements from South Carolina, who immediately wheel into line. The white 'Havelock' cap covers of the Carolinians are a typical feature of early Civil War dress, soon to be discarded for more versatile and less conspicuous slouch hats.

Surprise . . . due to their militia uniforms, the 33rd Virginia of the 'Stonewall Brigade' were mistaken by union commanders on Henry Hill for friendly troops, and were thus able to take a Federal battery by surprise attack.

Volley fire: though the muskets of the 1860s were normally rifled, and able to hit a man-sized target at 300 yards (twice the range of the smooth-bores of the Napoleonic era), Civil War commanders still relied on the effect of closely packed linear formations trading well-timed but individually unaimed volley- fire at close ranges. The unit of firepower was not the rifleman, but the company or regiment 'aimed and fired' by its officers. This was not only because individual marksmanship varied enormously; it was also necessary because after a few volleys the individual could no longer see his foe.

Gettysburg, July 1988 — the third day on Cemetery Ridge. In bright sunshine, the leading ranks of Pickett's Confederates charge towards the Union line.

The same engagement, seen from the Confederate ranks . . . As in the real battles of the 19th century, the black powder smoke of whole re-enactment regiments firing soon forms a dense, low-lying fog which hides friend and foe alike and even obscures the sun. Small wonder that generals of the Civil War did not place much trust in aimed infantry fire, but relied on massed volleys followed up with bayonet charges. At the 1988 Gettysburg re-enactment, as 125 years earlier, smoke and dust were so thick that everything was shrouded in a greyish haze, and flags were the only means of orientation in the chaos.

Acting up: Confederates taking part in a California re-enactment of Gettysburg buckle and fall in front of a Union position.

Skirmish lines, as demonstrated here by West German re-enactors, had only a limited tactical effect as screens in front of larger bodies of formed infantry.

Confederates from West Germany's '5th Virginia' club try to strike a suitable woebegone attitude during the re-enactment of the 1865 campaign.

German re-enactors, in the motley garb of recruits, struggle to master the intricacies of McClellan's bayonet fighting drill.

Another view of the National Regiment at Gettysburg, 1988, offering the sort of perspective that really can transport the spectator back in time momentarily. Commanded by Terry Daley of Maryland, the unit had a registered strength of no less than 867 infantrymen from many smaller groups.

Now, as then, the culmination of any encounter is the charge to capture the enemy's position. West Berlin's '1st Infantry Regiment' charge a Confederate roadblock in the Baumholder NATO training area.

The Old Camp Ground

Tent city: the sprawling canvas suburbs of a major re-enactment meeting, mostly made up of A-tents, accommodate thousands of participants and their families. At First Manassas in July 1986 it was calculated that 5,173 authentic period tents were erected; at Gettysburg in June 1988 this figure is believed to have been doubled.

Units are proud of the orderly appearance of their camps, forming their tent lines into company streets, as in the huge encampment at Gettysburg where men of the 7th Florida take their ease. Back in Florida, under the pines of Olustee, the neat lines of dog-tents made from shelter-halves by the 43rd North Carolina won prizes for authenticity of appearance.

While most re-enactors prefer the more spacious A-tents, the small 'dog-tents' (so christened by the soldiers of the Civil War because 'they would only accommodate a dog, and a small one at that') are more authentic. Re-enactors seldom sleep more than two to a tent, although in the 1860s four soldiers might share one of these. They offered less than complete protection from bad weather, since they were open at both ends. In the foreground is a fine example of the working replica arms industry: an Italian-made Navy Arms replica of the Model 1860 Henry rifle, the 16-shot, .44 cal. repeater which represented the most modern weapon in the Union arsenal. The replica uses modern .44-40 centrefire nitro cartridges instead of the old black powder rimfire loads of the original.

Some re-enactors are prepared to carry 'Living History' to considerable lengths, even preparing and cooking their food in the old style while they are in camp. Here men of a Union artillery battery offer advice — no doubt warmly appreciated — to a comrade happily engaged in disassembling fowls.

Time spent exploring the booths of the camp-followers is seldom wasted. There is always a crowd lining up at the photographer's wagon 'to have their likeness struck', and prints are supplied in convincing-looking 19th century styles and finishes.

Camp discipline; true to the period, a miscreant is drummed through the camp carrying heavy logs, a placard proclaiming his shame.

John A. Coffer, purveyor of ambrotypes and ferrotypes, talks dollars and cents with a bunch of Rebs while their comrade sits rigidly in front of the long-exposure lens.

Father and son encountered at Olustee in Union Navy outfits. In the 19th century many boys as young as this served aboard men-o'- war as 'powdermonkeys', running the powder cartridges from the fireproof magazines to the gun crews.

For sutlers such as Levi Ledbetter the actual battle re-enactments are the only time when their tented stores and booths are not mobbed by customers anxious to complete their outfits with ever more authentic items. Sutler's Row is also a good spot for beggars, invalids, entertainers, and mountebanks of every kind seeking to separate the honest soldier from his coin.

Some have turned re-enactment into a livelihood by joining the cottage industry catering for the needs of the 'Living History' endeavour. This carpenter deals from his officer's tent in authentic folding camp furniture, and less authentic, but equally welcome notions such as modern ice-boxes disguised in wooden chests.

'Living History' is a family affair in many instances; 'Fourth Bull Run' attracted no less than 1,200 women camp-followers and uncounted children. Since many wives have to sew their menfolks' uniforms, they consider that they might as well share the enjoyment of turning out in 19th century finery.

Some turn out as ladies of quality visiting the camps, some as laundresses or sutleresses. Since balls and barn dances have increasingly become a feature of the large re-enactment events, a touch of beauty and grace is seldom hard to find among the weekend warrior caste.

Command and Services

Sunrise at the headquarters of the Army of
Northern Virginia at Gettysburg, 1988,
with horse lines for officers and despatch
riders close by.

Nearby, specialists of the Signal Corps are busy with their 'talking flags' on a shaky-looking tower.

The Topographical Engineers are not just for show: they are actually employed in surveying and drawing up plans of the re-enactment area, camp grounds and the access roads.

General Robert E. Lee rides round the camps of the Army of Northern Virginia at Gettysburg, encouraging his loyal troops.

Attended by patient escorts, army commanders co-ordinate their plans for the battle to come.

An authentically dressed 'correspondent' rests against a split-rail breastwork at Gettysburg while he sketches a battlefield to illustrate his report to *Harper's Weekly*.

In the early morning mist Union and Confederate generals confer. At the Gettysburg anniversary event 34-year-old artist and antique dealer Michael Krause commanded the Federal forces; and 47-year-old Don Patterson, a builder of custom homes, led the army of the Confederacy. With a total of some 12,000 armed men, hundreds of horses and scores of cannon under command, their task was as genuinely demanding as that faced by many 1860s staff officers.

One of the specialised features which is increasingly to be seen at major events is a convincing Medical Department. While not all the 'wounded' carried off on litters are genuine, the medical staff are available to give first aid if needed. Generally, however, the 'sawbones' with their hospital tents, operating tables, and wicked-looking cased instruments are simply there as a reminder that war had a grim price in the 'good old days'. Here surgeons and their mates lay out their equipment ready for the flood of casualties; and an officer and soldier from the union Hospital Corps catch up on paperwork at Gettysburg — note orderly's green-trimmed jacket, the two styles of authentic chair, and the document chest which has a folding front to double as a writing desk.

A Confederate medical officer, in authentic green-faced uniform, confers with one of his nurses.

Confederate nurses recover wounded in the field.

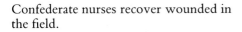

Cavalry —
Echo of a Distant Bugle

In the cool of dawn troopers of the 7th Illinois Volunteer Cavalry Regiment prepare to move out for drill at Gettysburg.

A 19TH CENTURY OFFICER is supposed to have remarked that cavalry added class to what would otherwise be a vulgar brawl. To this day the image of the dashing horseman with drawn sabre is wreathed in glamour and romance — though the Civil War reality was far removed from such sentimental abstractions. Despite the fact that the War Between the States was primarily an infantry rifleman's war, in the sense that the main engagements were decided by infantry, many re-enactors today are irresistibly drawn to join cavalry units even though the majority of these clubs are 'dismounted'. The prohibitive costs of maintaining horses and saddlery, and the demanding training programme necessary to shool rider and steed for 'war', prevent all but a very few Living History groups from turning out mounted. But where massed groups of horsemen do participate, the wild mock charges and flashing sabres never fail to focus the attention of spectators. The 1984 recreation of the historic cavalry action at Brandy Station, with some 200 mounted troopers, was thus a great step forward in the development of re-enactments.

First Manassas, 1986, saw only limited cavalry action due to the great heat and the broken nature of the terrain; nevertheless, 97 Confederate and 94 Union troopers took part on horseback. But the three-day Gettysburg event was highlighted by a real cavalry battle on 25 June 1988; this lasted close to three hours, with spirited charges and counter-charges by some 500 blue- and gray-clad horsemen, dismounted skirmish lines trading carbine fire, and massed artillery support.

Opposing the 'blue-bellies', dismounted skirmishers from Jeb Stuart's cavalry screen the bulk of the Confederate horsemen behind the rise. This engagement was to give the spectators an idea of the inconclusive clash between Stuart's and Gregg's cavalry corps on 3 July 1863, when 5,000 Union troopers prevented 7,000 Confederate horse from cutting behind Union lines at the same time as Pickett's infantry hammered at the Union centre on Cemetery Ridge.

overleaf
Opening moves on the third day at Gettysburg: using a small wood for cover, the dismounted skirmish line of C Troop, 7th Illinois open fire with their Sharps breech-loading carbines on advancing Confederate horse.

Jeb Stuart's first squadron rolls over the rise into the waiting lines of blue-clad troopers; and a spirited sabre mêlée breaks out around the Union guidon, resulting in empty saddles and a few cuts and bruises among the riders.

Returning from a vedette, a butternut-clad Texan cavalryman matches perfectly the popular image of the Southern cavalier.

Carbines at the ready, the second wave of Stuart's Confederate cavalry gather their horses for the advance into battle.

Sitting weary horses in strength-sapping heat, the 1st Virginia Cavalry wait for orders to move out. Note the original Maynard breech-loading carbine slung on a crossbelt. First Manassas, July 1986.

The cavalry camp, with tents set close to the horse lines; troopers loading cap-and-ball revolvers; and forage arriving in proper style by 'two horsepower' vehicle.

Virginia troopers, sabres in hand, during a pause in the battle of Gettysburg 1988. The uniforms may be reproduction, but the sun and dust are all too real.

Armed with an original Spencer seven-shot repeating carbine, this guidon-bearer from the 7th Illinois belongs to the best-equipped equestrian re-enactment group in the USA.

Early war cavalry: at the 1986 Manassas event the 7th Illinois posed as the peacetime regular 5th Cavalry, which in 1861 was still decked out in Hardee hats, dark blue trousers, and brass epaulettes.

Late war cavalry: at the Olustee event, Confederate horsemen from the 2nd Florida and 4th Georgia Cavalry represent the lean raider types of the 1864-65 period.

Most cavalry re-enactors share the fate of this California club: lacking mounts, they are obliged to fight on foot, using their carbines for vedette duties and flank cover.

Artillery — Rolling Thunder

LIKE THE DASHING CAVALRY, the artillery — with their roaring cannon, jingling six-horse teams, and smart red-trimmed uniforms — hold a fascination for the spectator which the infantry mass can seldom attract. But in the American Civil War the field pieces did not play the dominant rôle which they had boasted in Europe during the Napoleonic Wars; indeed, they accounted for only five per cent of battlefield casualties. This was largely due to the use of incorrect tactics, and the longer accurate range of rifled muskets. Lack of modern communications meant that artillery still had to fire directly and in line-of-sight at their targets; and this put them inside the range of aimed rifle fire, which could be concentrated on gun crews with deadly effect — for example, Berdan's Sharpshooters annihilated a battery of the élite Richmond Howitzers at the battle of Malvern Hill. More often than not the batteries were dispersed to support their infantry brigades.

The early re-enactments of the 1960s saw mostly one-third or one-half scale cannon, but these days major events permit only full-size ordnance. The rôle of an artillery re-enactor is hard work. While their historic counterparts could at least rely on horsepower to wheel the guns into action, the modern Civil War cannoneer has to manhandle his piece most of the time. Only a few fortunate groups can afford the six-horse team (or, at least, a mule team) to draw limber and cannon during a re-enactment. But the rewards in terms of public acclaim can be sweet: few sights draw cheers from the spectators like a horsedrawn gun team pulling up and wheeling into position, unlimbering with practised speed, crashing off a few shots, and then hitching up to dash off to another part of the field.

overleaf
Union four-gun battery blasting away at the advancing Confederate lines during the re-enactment of Pickett's charge at Gettysburg, 1988. Billowing smoke clouds are often enhanced by ramming a couple of pounds of flour down on top of the powder charge in place of a roundshot.

Battery D, 5th United States Artillery Regiment photographed at Fredericksburg on 3 May 1863 during the Chancellorsville campaign. (Library of Congress)

Modern artillery teams rely upon mechanised horsepower and flatbed trailers to get their guns to the battlefield. Once there, hauling the ordnance into position is a matter of human muscle — and a 3in. 'Ordnance rifle' ten-pounder weighs around half a ton.

Only a few clubs can afford to own or rent a full team of six horses to pull gun and limber. In 1986 at Manassas two re-enactment artillery clubs acting as regular Union army horse artillery added realism to the event by constantly switching the positions of their two pieces.

Resting on the wheel of an original 12-pdr. at the Antietam battlefield, this well-dressed corporal belongs to a Living History group employed by the National Park Service during the summer months as 'interpreters', to give visitors 'first person' accounts of the battles and army life of the 1860s. He is holding the 'worm' which was used to draw charges from the cannon barrel.

In the Civil War every battery had its own travelling forge, drawn by a six-horse team like the guns and caissons. This smith, with his authentically rebuilt forge, is a sure crowd-puller at re-enactments; but he is also a much-needed trader, supplying all kinds of iron hardware to re-enactors.

The group also demonstrate period gun drill, and here stand in the correct positions for the crew at the beginning of the sequence. Crew members, from left to right in this photo, are: No.1, standing right of muzzle with sponge/rammer staff; No.3 behind him; No.2, standing left of muzzle; the corporal 'chief of piece'; No.4, behind No.2; No.5, with slung pouch; No.6, by ammunition chest from limber, well to rear; and the sergeant commanding two guns.

On the command '*Load*' No.1 sponges out the barrel; No.5 takes a load from No.6, who has cut fuse to length as ordered, and carries it in his pouch up to No.2. No.2 puts it in the muzzle, and No.1 rams it home while No.3 covers the touch-hole with his thumb to prevent the air stream re-igniting sparks from the last shot. No.3 then aims the gun with a handspike, at the orders of the corporal. When satisfied, the latter steps aside, and shouts '*Ready*'. Nos. 1 and 2 step out of the way of the recoil and the muzzle blast; No.3 pricks the cartridge bag through the touch-hole; No.4 hooks a lanyard to a friction primer and inserts it in the touch-hole; No.3 covers this with his hand to prevent premature discharge; No.4 moves out to the side with the lanyard. On the order '*Fire*' No.3 steps clear and No.4 pulls the lanyard, while the sergeant and 'chief of piece' observe the fall of shot. A practised crew can get off two or three rounds a minute.

Confederate gunners of the Richmond Howitzers, an élite and well-equipped militia artillery company, take a break during gun drill at the tent camp during 'Fourth Bull Run'.

No.4 in the gun team; and a fellow Southern artillery 'number'. It is not all that unusual to discover women re-enactors in the ranks of artillery units.

'*Ready!*' — the No.4 of an 1861 3in. 10-pdr. 'Ordnance rifle' holds slack the lanyard to the friction-pull primer, waiting the final order.

A first sergeant of Garrison Artillery from the Living History group based at Fort Point underneath San Francisco's Golden Gate bridge. He wears peacetime full dress uniform with Hardee hat, brass scale epaulettes, and the Roman-style M1833 artillery shortsword.

The largest piece at 'Fourth Bull Run' was this majestic brass 20-pdr. of 1840 vintage.

12-pdr. gun-howitzers lined up with their limbers in the Centreville camp during the 1986 Manassas re-enactment — in which no less than 54 pieces of ordnance took part. Each cost between $3,500 and $5,500, without counting the many accessories.

Live firing: a Yankee gun-captain squints through the brass sight of his 10-pdr. Parrott gun during the 200 yard target competition on the North-South Skirmish Association range at Fort Shenandoah. In a battle re-enactment there would be no question of his displaying such modern touches as the ticket and the wristwatch.

In large re-enactments such as the 125th anniversary series a whole group of pyrotechnical experts provide the explosive back-up in the target area, to make the artillery fire look even more convincing. A lot of work in the hot sun goes into each of the holes for the spectacular radio-detonated ground-bursts. For air-bursts something akin to a baby *Katyusha* rocket-launcher is used from behind cover to lob one-pound bags of explosives and magnesium high into the air above the warring battle lines.

The North-South Skirmish Association

IT IS NOT ONLY because of their veteran status within the re-enactment community that the N-SSA enjoys a special rôle among Civil War hobby groups. The organisation's declared purpose is 'to conduct skirmishes in our traditional form of company target competition. To promote muzzle-loading rifle shooting through the use of Civil War weapons fired in the original manner, and to encourage the preservation and display of Civil War material. To commemorate the heroism of the men of both sides who fought in the Civil War, 1861-65, as a reminder of our national heritage.'

The organisation which grew out of that first shooting contest in May 1950 has today developed into a nationwide association with some 3,300 active members. With such numbers, and with two annual competitions — the 'Nationals' in May and October — normal club ranges have long ceased to be adequate. In 1963 the members pooled their resources and bought a huge, sprawling area near Winchester on the Virginia/West Virginia border. A small wooded valley off the Shenandoah Valley, with a clear mountain stream running down its centre, it accommodates ranges on one side and a camping area on the other.

'Fort Shenandoah' is now the single largest range in the whole United States. On a 500-yard-long firing line 50 teams each of eight members can blast away at the targets shoulder to shoulder. The same range, used lengthways, allows clubs to fire their original and reproduction field pieces at 100 and 200 yards.

All firing is done with weapons from the Civil War — rifle-muskets, cap-and-ball revolvers, or breech-loading carbines; and every one of the Nationals includes a black powder cannon and mortar competition. Unlike modern black powder sport shooting, all loading is from the belt pouch or slung ammo box, with either pre-rolled paper cartridges or small plastic charger tubes holding powder and ball.

Paper 'bullseye' targets are considered too boring, so the team competitions use clay pots, ceramic tiles or clay pigeons as used in trap shooting. The idea is to clean out a line of these satisfying targets at 50 or 100 yards by rapid fire. The contest consists of four or five stages each of 360 seconds. In each stage 16 or 32 targets have to be hit by each eight-man team. The winner is the team which destroys all its targets in the shortest time.

These competitions are a sight to be seen. With 400 muskets going off at the sound of the starting gong the range immediately fills up with smoke, and the din is indescribable. With each shooter firing an average ten rounds per stage, the backstop is filled with some 250 pounds weight of lead in each six-minute shoot-out.

Though the N-SSA members consider themselves shooters first, they strive for a traditional appearance. All shooting has to be done in authentic garb, and each team has to represent a real unit from the Civil War. The Nationals are enlivened by barbecues, and balls in historical dress.

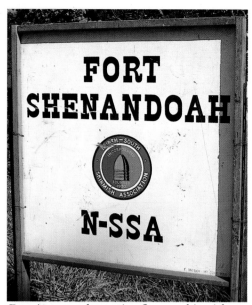

Burning powder grains fly as a skirmisher blasts away at the distant clay targets.

The huge firing line at Fort Shenandoah cuts loose with the first volley.

A Confederate skirmisher draws a bead during a carbine team competition, while his comrade bites the cartridge for his next musketoon round.

Cartridges ready to hand and rifle-musket primed, a Union skirmisher waits tensely for the firing-gong.

A Confederate skirmisher carefully blackens the sights on his original Maynard .50 cal. breech-loading carbine.

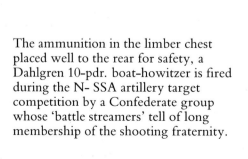

The ammunition in the limber chest placed well to the rear for safety, a Dahlgren 10-pdr. boat-howitzer is fired during the N- SSA artillery target competition by a Confederate group whose 'battle streamers' tell of long membership of the shooting fraternity.

On the artillery gun-line: the lanyard is ripped away with a flourish, and the piece bellows.

Using the traditional method of string alignment, members of the 3rd US Artillery prepare their 8in. M1861 mortar.

Laying their gun for the 200 yard precision shoot, Union gunners use the traditional aiming devices on their muzzle-loader.

Val Forgett, owner of the famous Navy Arms replica company, is a veteran N-SSA member and an artillery buff; here he joins the competition with an original M1861 Krupp breech-loader.

Slow match burning, the team steps aside from a piece fired by linstock (rather than by friction primer and lanyard) to watch the strike of the solid shot on the target.

On the way! A 3in. gun belches smoke and fire.